Pebble® Plus

Hands-On Science Fun

How to Make a LIQUID RAINBOW

Revised Edition

by Lori Shores

Consultant: Ronald Browne, PhD
Department of Elementary & Early Childhood Education
Minnesota State University, Mankato

Download the
Capstone 4D app
for additional content.

 See page 2
for directions.

CAPSTONE PRESS
a capstone imprint

Download the Capstone 4D app!

- Ask an adult to search in the Apple App Store or Google Play for "Capstone 4D".
- Click Install (Android) or Get, then Install (Apple).
- Open the app.
- Scan any of the following spreads with this icon:

When you scan a spread, you'll find fun extra stuff to go with this book! You can also find these things on the web at www.capstone4D.com using the password: **rainbow.09465**

Pebble Plus is published by Capstone Press,
1710 Roe Crest Drive, North Mankato, Minnesota 56003
www.mycapstone.com

Library of Congress Cataloging-in-Publication Data
is available on the Library of Congress website.

ISBN 978-1-5435-0946-5 (library binding)
ISBN 978-1-5435-0952-6 (paperback)
ISBN 978-1-5435-0958-8 (ebook pdf)

Editorial Credits
Marissa Kirkman, editor; Sarah Bennett, designer; Tracy Cummins, media researcher; Tori Abraham, production specialist

Photo Credits
Capstone Studio: Karon Dubke, Cover, 3, 5, 7, 9, 11, 13, 15, 17, 19, 21; Shutterstock: Elina Lif, 1, Design Element, golubok, Cover Background, irin-k, 4-5 Background

Note to Parents and Teachers

The Hands-On Science Fun set supports national science standards related to physical science. This book describes and illustrates how to make a liquid rainbow. The images support early readers in understanding the text. The repetition of words and phrases helps early readers learn new words. This book also introduces early readers to subject-specific vocabulary words, which are defined in the Glossary section. Early readers may need assistance to read some words and to use the Table of Contents, Glossary, Read More, Internet Sites, Critical Thinking Questions, and Index sections of the book.

Printed and bound in the United States of America.
010772S18

Table of Contents

Getting Started 4

Making a Liquid Rainbow 6

How Does It Work? 16

Glossary 22

Read More 23

Internet Sites 23

Critical Thinking Questions 24

Index 24

Safety Note:
Please ask an adult for help when making a liquid rainbow.

Getting Started

Rainbows reach across the sky. You can build a liquid rainbow in a jar.

Here's what you need:

½ cup (120 mL)
light corn syrup

½ cup (120 mL)
blue dish soap

½ cup (120 mL)
water

½ cup (120 mL)
olive oil

½ cup (120 mL)
rubbing alcohol

3 mugs

1-quart (1-liter) jar

spoon

red, blue, and green
food coloring

5

Making a Liquid Rainbow

Pour ½ cup corn syrup into a mug.

Stir in 1 drop each of blue and red food coloring.

Pour the purple corn syrup
into a jar.

Next, slowly pour ½ cup
blue dish soap into the jar.

Pour ½ cup water
into another mug.

Stir in 2 drops of
green food coloring.

Tilt the jar. Very slowly pour
the green water along the inside
of the jar.

Then, slowly pour ½ cup
olive oil into the jar.

In another mug, stir 2 drops
red food coloring into
½ cup rubbing alcohol.
Tilt the jar and very slowly
pour in the rubbing alcohol.

Stand back and take a look.
Do you see a rainbow?

How Does It Work?

Liquids are made up of very tiny particles. How tightly packed these particles are determines density. Dish soap floats on corn syrup because the soap is less dense.

You carefully poured the water

so it wouldn't mix with the soap.

Water is less dense than dish soap.

The water floated on top.

Not all liquids can mix.

The oil didn't mix with the water.

Did the rubbing alcohol mix
with the oil?

Which one was denser?

Glossary

density—how closely packed particles are in a liquid or in an object

liquid—a wet substance that can be poured

particle—a very small piece of something

tilt—to tip to one side

Read More

Brunelle, Lynn. *Big Science for Little People: 52 Activities to Help You and Your Child Discover the Wonders of Science.* Boulder, Colo.: Roost Books, 2016.

Citro, Asia. *The Curious Kid's Science Book: 100+ Creative Hands-On Activities for Ages 4–8.* Woodinville, Wash.: Innovative Press, 2015.

Sohn, Emily. *Experiments in Earth Science and Weather with Toys and Everyday Stuff.* Fun Science. North Mankato, Minn.: Capstone Press, 2016.

Internet Sites

Use FactHound to find Internet sites related to this book.

Visit *www.facthound.com*

Just type **9781543509465** and go.

 **Super-cool stuff!** Check out projects, games and lots more at **www.capstonekids.com**

Critical Thinking Questions

1. What are liquids made up of?

2. What determines the density of a liquid?

3. Which liquid was the most dense? How do you know?

Index

corn syrup, 6, 8, 16
density, 16, 18, 20
dish soap, 8, 16, 18
floating, 16, 18
food coloring, 6, 10, 14
liquids, 4, 16, 20

mixing, 18, 20
olive oil, 12, 20
particles, 16
rubbing alcohol, 14, 20
water, 10, 12, 18, 20